MW01659777

M.O.P

Ministry on Paper Presents...

Kill I

Lawrence Washington Jr.

Library of Congress Control Number: 2011945195

ISBN: 978-0-9849360-1-4

Cover Design: Brittany J. Jackson

Published by G Publishing, LLC

Printed in the United States of America

Dedication

I would like to dedicate this book to my cousins, Robert Montgomery (Gooba) & Devon McCaskill (Moonie). I love you, and I thank God for the years we had together. You will always be missed and remembered…

Acknowledgments

I want to first thank the greatest Poet in all creation, My Lord and Savior Jesus Christ. He gave me the gift of poetry and helped me to discover this gift during my lonely season in life (before I received Him into my heart). Without Him I wouldn't exist. I want to thank my queen, my friend, my laughing buddy, my gift from God, a.k.a. my Wife. You put up with me the most when I would practice my poems all day long. Thank you for being my best friend. I also want to thank my mother for always encouraging and pushing me to finish this project. She would tell everybody that her son has a book coming out every year. (And I didn't want to make her a liar so it pushed me to this point.) I want to thank my father, for having so much patience with me when I would read my poems over and over to him to practice my presentation. He is an awesome critic. I have the greatest parents in the world. I want to thank my sisters, Taroza and Toya, for believing in my gift. Thank you, Taroza for creating opportunities for me to exercise my gift and meet other great poets. Toya, thank you for listening to my poems over the phone and for having a heartwarming response every time. I love my sisters sooo much. I want to thank my oldest daughter,

Hailey for being my biggest fan. She loves to listen to her daddy's voice over and over again. I want to thank my Church family for always encouraging me to keep citing my poems. I want to thank everyone who appreciates the gift God has given me, and encouraged me along the way. I can't say thank you enough, may God continue to Bless each and everyone of you.

Thank you.

Table of Contents

"I am nothing but He is everything. Me is wrapped in Thee, so the only way I can be something is to let the Something of Something come into my Nothing and Live. JIS-Jesus is Something and I am Nothing without Jesus."

—Pastor Seon Thompson

Kill I

Introduction

'Kill I' is my feature poem because it is the focal point in my life. When I gave my life to Christ, he allowed me to see and understand that it is not about me, and it never was. It's all about God, His will, His desire, and His pleasure. This poem was inspired by a dream. When I started writing this poem I finished it in about 10 min. I hope you are blessed by it. I cite this poem whenever I feel myself loosing focus on this truth... He must increase, but I must decrease. (St. John 3:30)

Kill I

Close your eyes
And realize the disguise
Of a trap
Waiting to capture you
Into the pits of failure and distress
Go ahead and confess
Your weakness to the strongest, kindest
Most powerful, brightest
And most loving spirit
And open your ears
For when He speaks
You are able to hear Him
Come out from behind those invisible curtains
And fulfill your purpose…
These are the words addressed to I
On my life's journey
I am constantly reminded of how blinded
I have become
God is waiting for I to die
Because I can't reside
In His Kingdom
Not by Satan
But I am blinded by I
My eyes must be closed
For God has allowed me to understand that

I am the one He has chose
Clothes
Do not define I
Doors
Cannot continue to slide
Open
If I continue to live life only hoping
To reach Him up high
Read more of His word must I
Let Him dwell in me must I
Do His will willingly must I
And fall to my knees
And ask Him to
Help me please (3 xs)
Must I
And discard the phrase
When things get hard
"Lord why me"
Must I
While He sits back and sigh
Knowing that it is not Him
But it is I
The guy who walks side by side
Without fighting I

Because he is too busy using his own useless might

And falls and cries
After he realize
That he is weak without Me
But strong without I…

You see it's time for I to die!
And the lamp to be lit inside
Because without I
There is no pride
Without I
There is no fall
Only me standing upright and tall
Without I
There is no weakness but meekness
No wicked desires
No path leading to the fire
No hesitation for praise and veneration
Without I
There is no hypocrisy
Life is no mystery
And misery becomes history
Without I
There is no confusion

And being delivered from all my sins
Is
NOT A DELUSION!

So no more words are there to say to I but
Bye Bye
For I am now a new guy
Who has only one main goal in life
Which is to live by the word
And die by the word
With God on my side
All because I want to meet Him high in the sky
So I say to I
Bye Bye
And I say to I
Bye Bye
Yes I say to I
Bye Bye
And I lift up holy hands with much faith
Knowing that
Even if He doesn't do it for me
I know He can
And I is banned
From my Holy Temple
And I lift up holy hands
Again

With thanksgiving
For allowing me to
Close my eyes
And realize the disguise

Of a trap
Waiting to capture me
Into the pits of failure and distress
I have confessed
My weakness
To the strongest
Kindest
Most powerful
Brightest
And most loving spirit
And my ears are now open
For when He speaks
I am now able to hear him
I came out from behind those invisible curtains
And I am ready to fulfill my purpose
So therefore I lift up Holy Hands
Why?
Because- I –have- finally –died…
Today…
But tomorrow
I-must-die
Again…

Vanity

Vanity of Vanity, all is vanity says the preacher…
We're living this life to
Please men twice, all by the desire of being
wanted
So we find ourselves stuck in the middle
Between death
Our shell,
And the breath
Of fresh air
Trying all the day long
To fill in that void
That's been created since birth
Affected by the choices we make
Neglected in the situation
After the choices we have made
We fight and fight
To try and grab hold
And take control
But we can't…
As we fail to realize
That we've already had the chance
To control the only thing given to us to do
freely
Not realizing
The significance of my Lord and Savior dying…
On the cross…
For the lost…

The paid cost
Made necessary to make us free
To do what benefits us the most
Which is choosing to pursue the desire of our soul!
By hearing God's word
Believing God's word
And receiving the most valuable
Powerful, Influential, Commanding,
Authoritative, Controlling, Dominant,
Great, potent, and undeserved gift given by the God almighty,
Through his son Jesus Christ, called the
Holy Ghost!
So that we can live a holy life
And please don't judge me and think that I am trying to preach
But I only said that
For those who don't know...
Now to get back on track
Have you ever sat back
And considered
That
Even the famous and rich are bitter
Although
It might seem different on TV
But I guarantee you
It's a different story behind the scenes
But
Enough about them

Because my goal
Is not to inform you about them
And give a nice Poetry show
Because it's not about me
It's all about Him
I just want the whole World to know
That Life is Vanity
If you put your life before the Almighty
Life is Vanity
If you put Jim before him
And don't think I only said Jim because Jim
rhymes with him
But Jim represents all the natural earthly things
We put before the reason of our being
Whether it be
He or she
The clothes on our back
The shoes on our feet
The jobs we work in order to eat
The food we eat
The jewelry
Our own self-esteem
What we think
What we gain intellectually
What we do got
What we aint got
Where we hang at
What we crave
What we want so we can flaunt
What we want so we can no more want

I can go on and on
Until the break of dawn
But you all will be sleep
And thinking to yourselves that this long list is all vanity…

I hope you can now see
That if I continue on and on trying to reach
My goal
To teach
And show
You vanity
By talking till you feel the warmth in your seat
Or the pain in your feet
That it would be all vanity…
Now to shine the light off of me
And on to you
Can you now see?
When you put your life before Christ
Day in and day out
You might as well stop and quit
Because if you don't receive and pursue Christ in your life
(In which he himself has given you)
Your candle is not lit
And without the fire
Your soul's desire has not been met
While rejecting the Truth
That Christ is longing to be loved by You
And you aint got to give any thing but your life

He will accept you and he won't think twice
So if you are living this life
Searching for love in all the wrong places
I hope your eyes can now see
But if you can't
Please read
The 12th chapter of Ecclesiastes
So
When you are searching to fill in that void
that's been Created since birth
While putting your life before Christ
It is all
Vanity of vanity
All is Vanity says the preacher…

Hollow Thoughts

Hollow thoughts continue to travel in the mind
Of a young man who is trying
To understand God's plan for his life

He feels he has no choice but to think twice
To the 10th power
But as the next hour approaches
His thoughts began to grow faster than ghetto house roaches

He then began to be elated
And starts to think a little bit faster
All thanks to the works of the food he just ate and
Because he can still taste it
He then starts writing what has been
In his mind on black & white paper

Feeling higher than a skyscraper
He releases what has caused him to hurt for no reason
Move slower than a winter season
And think of everyone as heathens
But wow
He now
Speaks to anyone that walks in his path
He no longer has to give out a fake laugh

He stays genuine like a man's mother
A much sincere heart is now created
Everyone around him is blessed
And inspired by his thoughts on paper
He gives thanks to the Almighty
Because He's good
And He does nothing to try and hurt us
And most of all for helping him
In discovering that his thoughts on paper
Is his Purpose...

Living my Life

I'm living my life!
To please God only
Because I know with Him I could never become lonely.

I'm living my Life!
To treat others with respect
Because I do not want to become one of God's rejects

I'm living my life!
To pray for my sisters and brothers as well as for others

I'm living my life!
To find the right woman
So we can grow together and to have a chance to say that "I found a Good Thang"
And as of August 16th, 2008
I can proudly say
That
"I found a good thang"

I'm living my life!
To put smiles on many faces
While traveling to many places
Beyond the basics

I'm living my life!
To help change lives
And I wouldn't mind
Helping to
Save marriages between husband and wives

I'm living my life!
To witness
By giving God all the credit because...
(Like the song writer said)
"I'm just a nobody, trying to tell everybody
About somebody
Who can save anybody"

I'm living my life!
Because I know my purpose
So don't live yours fooling yourself about not being perfect
By hiding behind invisible curtains

I'm living my life!
I'm living my Life!
I'm living my Life yall!

For Jesus...
So please get a clue
And live yours too

Because tomorrow is not promised
And
Just like Uncle Sam
Jesus Christ wants you!

That's why I'm living my life…

Lord Please Help Me!!!

David said it best
He was so good at crying out in times of distress
What shall I do Lord?
How do I deal with the feeling of being alone in
my own home?
Lord please help me!
Help me find the answer
This mess is eating away at me like sickness
cancer
I try to block it off
I hope to brush it off but
Satan is like a busy bee
Working diligently daily
Trying to keep me from reaching my spiritual
peak
Lord Please Help Me!
I need you
Open my understanding
Help my wife to better understand me
Open up my eyes so that I might see
That she really does care for me
And open up her eyes that she may see
That all I want is for her just to acknowledge me
Just to hold me, just to love me...
Lord please---- Help me...

Why Do I Feel This Way?

(My first poem)

Why do I feel this way?
What is this feeling inside of me that keeps burning day after day?
Is it depression?
Or will it be a life learned lesson?
Lord I'm just guessing...

When I wake up
I feel so incomplete
And I don't know why
Because
My life is great
And I got shoes on my feet
My family is strong
And I have a great home
So
Lord-Lord-Lord
Please just tell me what's wrong
I need an uplifting song
For you have
Given me this burning desire
And it's
Just like fire
Shut up in my bones
This feeling
Refuses to leave me alone

And
I know it's you Lord
I can feel you inside of me
And the more I write
You help me to realize
That it's not all about me...
It's all about you Lord
For you've helped me to realize
You are the one
I need to seek more of
For you have blessed me with life
And you continue to show me so much love...
So
No longer will I ask the question
"Why?"
Again
I can now accept the desire
To be saved from sin
For you have sent your son to die
On the cross for my sins
And rise again
Can I get an AAMEN...?
I can now thank you lord
For this
Burning fire
For I am now a worker for you
That won't even think

To retire
Now I know why
I felt that way…

Twenty Two Years

Twenty Two years of Growth
Twenty Two years of sharing jokes
Twenty two years of
Not just breaking,
But together
Destroying yokes
Twenty two years of ups and downs
Twenty two years of smiles and frowns
I'm so glad that my daddy has found
A wonderful woman like this one
Ask my sisters, I'm sure they'd agree
But don't ask my brother because I'm the only son
And you've already heard it from me...

Listen

My parents have been through a lot
Through the thick and thin
Throughout my entire life
I have never seen them practice sin
Concerning discipline
They didn't need any help
They didn't believe in time outs
So they just used my deddy's paint belt!
They are parents of three children
Always willing to help others

So they adopted one more
This now makes them parents of four
My father is always relaxed
Cool, smooth, and quick to laugh
My mother…
Well she's the total opposite
This is why they are able to make it
Through any obstacle
That comes their way
Bankruptcy, they been there
Confusion, they overcame it
Arguments, they settled them
Problems, they solved
Their spirituality throughout the years
Have evolved
Their marriage
Has evolved
They are one!
They are the one couple that has the ability to look Satan in his face
Stand straight up and say

"We have overcome!
All the test and trials that came our way
We are one, under the sun;
With three girls and one son

We have won
So therefore we are one…"

And when they are done
We can look at them and be happy
And celebrate with them

Twenty Two years of Growth
Twenty two years of sharing jokes
Twenty two years of...
Not just breaking
But together
Destroying yokes
Twenty two years of ups and downs
Twenty two years of smiles and frowns
I'm so glad that my deddy has found
A wonderful woman like this one
Ask my sisters, I'm sure they'd agree
But don't ask my brother because I'm the only son
And you've already heard it from me...
Full of glee
When I look and see
Two wonderful people together make it through 22 years
Makes me stand to my feet
And realize that this can happen to you and me
Without fear, but with the woman I will find...
Because God has created the spirit of Love, Power, and a Sound mind

Congratulations momma and daddy
Pastor Lawrence Washington Sr.
And first Lady,
Missionary Donna F. Washington after
Twenty-Two-Years

The Prayer of Patience

It seems like all the good ones
Are taken accept me
I must have patience so that I can find
The right one
Who can respect herself and most of all
Respect me
It's a good thing you've created
Patience Lord
Because without it
I'll fall in love with anyone
And probably think nothing about it
So I am going to keep searching to find
The one that I can put my all in
She has to have the same goal as me
Which is to increase in you
And the desire to be saved from sin
I can now thank you Lord
For teaching me such a valuable lesson
I just can't rush and expect to find my blessing...
Amen.

My Soul Mate

Introduction

'My Soul Mate' was written for my godmother. She wanted me to write a poem dedicated to her husband as they renewed their wedding vowels after 25 years. This poem was written to express the way she felt about him. She took the time to express to me her feelings and thoughts toward him, and I transformed her feelings and thoughts into a poem. Plainly speaking, this poem is from a woman to her husband, in particular.

<u>My Soul Mate</u>

Such a great amount of Grace
Have been given unto me
According to my life's fate
Because God has Blessed me
In the nineteenth century
At a young age
In my youthful days
With my soul mate.

First he saved my soul
And he made me whole
Placed my feet on a solid ground
Filled me with the Holy Ghost
And because his grace is so great
He has blessed me with my soul mate.

Now I didn't have much as a child
And before I was old enough to
Get loose and run wild
God's love was great towards me
In 1983
And because his grace is so great
He has united me with my soul mate.

Yes, we started out young and in love
And today I stand to say
That our love goes Deep!

For I knew he was the one.

And today I stand to say
That even if our love was the deep blue sea
Our love would go so deep that another man
Would drown in the shallow end
Of our love
But I can swim in our love
Because I am able to enjoy our love
And today I stand to say
That after all these years
I can still appreciate
The presence of my Love
For my heart becomes so elated
And joy flows in like a flood
And my body becomes warm again
Similar to the day I became born again
Whenever I feel the embrace
Of-his-strong-black
Hands
When I receive just one...
Hug from my love
And today I stand to say
That my faithfulness goes deeper than
The symbolization of a wedding band...
(Even though it looks good on my hand)
For I have been so secure in my love

Since way back when he took my hand
Today I say

While I stand
"This is my man!!"
And because I came from his rib
That makes me his
wo-man.

And today I stand
With such a great amount of gratitude
Toward God's grace upon me
The thought of it makes me want to sing
And if I was to sing a song it would be...

"He saved my soul
And he made me whole
He placed my feet on a solid ground
He filled me with the Holy Ghost
And because his grace is so great
He has blessed me with my soul mate"

And today I stand to say
That it's because of God's grace
Our love is not able to be erased
This is why we are
Soul Mates.

The Vowel

The closer I get to you Lord
The more Satan attacks my mind
But much more you choose to remind
Me
That salvation is mine
And all power is in your hands
When friends are nowhere to be found
During times of sorrow
I can always count on you
Never have I thought to turn away
Because you've never promised tomorrow
Your Great knowledge, understanding, and
wisdom
I will follow
Thank you father
I shall look no further
I will continue to seek after you
I will continue to seek after you
Even Now
With my head bowed
This is my vowel

A New Man

Halleluiah!
I once was lost but now I'm found
My mind was once troubled but now its sound
I once walked around with a frown but now it's
turned upside down
I once was a fighter naturally
But now I am a fighter spiritually
I am now blessed lyrically
I now have a place in the tree
Of Life
And when the time is present to do his will
I will no longer think twice
I have a new name
For I am no longer the same
And I am blessed with favor
All thanks to my savior
For his plan considers myself
Filled with love and wealth
I am no longer Satan's fan
I have a new plan
That lines up with God's plan
This allows me to say that I am
A New Man!

The Recovery

Trials and tribulations
Dumb decisions are followed by consequences
Disappointment is created
No one is elated
While I sit and tear up
All because I've messed up
"Cheer up"
As my god momma says,
"Gotta keep ya head up"
Even though it's hard to disregard
Disappointing
Very important people in my life
My mentality is stronger
And I can't wait for them to see the increased hunger
The fight will continue
The battle is already won
No more having just fun
No more do I feel trapped like a hot dog in a bun
Ready for life's journey
Thanks for the wake-up call
A kick in the face and disgrace
Will not occur for a long time
It could be worse
Although I did commit a crime
Blindly taking things for granted
I'm anxious for this conviction to pass by

Soon I will become a successful guy
That will strive to keep someone else from
Making the same mistake I've made
Before I die...

Defeating the Cycle

The cycle is created through the danger behind sin
Folks are too busy depending on certain friends
Who cannot always lend a helping hand
And
Too blind to find the true meaning of life's purpose
Too scared so they hide behind glass curtains
Waiting to be exposed
Hoping for an escape
Or to find someone who can relate
To the pain that is gained
From the effort to be the same
Instead of living an individual life
Failure arise and contentment cascades
And then they become lost in their ways
And reality fades away, away, away
And the only hope is one touch of Love
From the Almighty God
And a touch understanding
Of the pain that was gained
From the sins committed of course
And no more sadness felt
All because the price was paid of course
Now able to free themselves
From living in hell but
Constantly chooses to be locked-up

As if the sacrifice was not enough
Finding themselves back at square one
Lying in a jail cell with the doors wide open...
(Selah)
You see the cycle continues and it must be destroyed
But it takes more than just a magic potion
The solution cannot be avoided
Right decisions must be made
Righteousness must be gained
It can all be done
In Jesus name
And by the help of his disciples
That is bold enough to stand up
And assist in
Defeating the cycle...

My Gift

Introduction

This poem was written as a proposal to my wife. I read it openly to her at a formal holiday banquet. She was sitting in a chair thinking she was representing Poetry. She had no idea that she was the gift until the end of the poem...

My Gift

(The proposal)

A gift has been given from God to me
In disguise before my eyes could see
That my gift was made especially for me

My gift keeps me on my feet and knees
Because I seek and seek
To find ways to encourage my gift
To lift up gift
To put a smile on the face of my gift
And when my gift is weak
I want to be there to strengthen my gift
To hold my gift
Hug and squeeze my gift
To love my gift

The beauty of my gift is so real
I just want to hold my gift so close to my heart
That not even the chief of thieves could steal
My gift away from me

I am so happy because so soon
God has decided to allow me to receive
The gift he has created just for me.

You may ask "how do I know it's my gift?"
Well he has blessed me to be able to see inside my gift.

Yes
He has blessed me to be the only one
On this earth to see the inner beauty that
Lies inside of my gift

My gift makes me complete
My gift will soon be a part of me
I am so full of glee
Which is why I love and appreciate my gift

Once again I say
A gift has been given from God to me
In disguise before my eyes could see
That my gift was made especially for me
In appreciation
I lift my voice without a slight hesitation
And I thank my God
For the gift that he has placed into my life without a cost
And because my gift is here tonight
I want her to stand up and look me straight into my eyes

While I stare into your eyes
And began to ask you the question that I've
Been waiting so long to ask
(As though it seems)

On one knee
LaToya Shanee Ross

Will You Marry Me?
(She said yes!)

My Love

Introduction

This poem was written to my wife before we united in marriage. I site this poem in weddings.

My Love

I'm feeling so warm inside
While thinking of you
Your smile
Is a manifestation of your character
Bright, consistent, and real
Is what my eyes can see
Your beauty is so well-built
That you'll even
Make the man of steel become weak in the knees
And please understand
That this is what my eyes can see
You have caused unknown feelings inside of me
To rise up and be
Transformed into the stars
Not in the sky
But the stars in my eyes...
I can't help but to say I love you
I love you for you
I can't wait to say on that day
"You are officially mine"
I will be officially yours and
The doors shall be open
That's when
We can do what we do and not sin and
Another door shall be open
We will enter in and
A whole new level of happiness shall began

Instantly we shall soon realize that
Our love will never come to an end
Through the storm and rain our love will
Glow white like the winter fresh snow
Giving others a chance to see
The love that flows and creates the glow
My Love for you will go so deep
That others will drown in my love for you but
I wish not to drown you in my love
I want to teach you how to swim in my love
Float on my love...
Because drowning leads to death and
I want you to feel my love
Experience my love
See my love
And my love
I want you to know that you are
My Love...

Peace on Earth

Peace on earth?
Man
We living as dirt!
Fed up with the innocent getting hurt and
Lying in a Hurst
There's no age limit and
The numbers keep rising
I wish this was a gimmick and
No one's fighting
Everyone's killing and
Unable to control an angry feeling
Lord how much will you tolerate?
This world is full of so much hate
The streets are full of crime
No one's doing the time
Until after the 10th lost life
The answer we must find
Someone should step up and
Seize an attitude that's kind
We need more gratitude
We need more nice people
Love is Lethal
But Lord how much will you tolerate?
Lust is rising
It's the cause of most people dying
Parents are lying
To their children for no apparent reason

Folks are walking around with a face
That yells out Hate!
An attitude that yells out Fake!
No one wants to communicate
Everyone decides to separate
No one stops to meditate
Everybody decides to take
Negativity in this society is embraced
Not many souls decide to focus
On what's positive for goodness sake!
Today I stand to say
Lord, Lord, Lord how long will you tolerate...

Parent Appreciation

Where do I start?
Straight from my heart
My parents have been there for me
Way back before I could stand on my own two feet... literally
Way back before I was able to crawl on my hands and knees
And because of you Lord!
My parents have provided me with all my needs
Even before I knew I had needs.

I'm just sitting, thinking, and thanking God for my parents

Now I'm thinking about the time
When they would whip my behind
Whenever I would be disobedient, disrespectful, stealing, destructive,
Or get caught telling a natural lie
I could never understand Why
(Before each whipping)
They would make me go get ***'The Belt'***
And I could not even lie at that time
And say "The Belt I can't find"
Because it was always the same belt and it was in the same place every time...
But on the flip side

Every time they whip me
They helped me to see my wrong
And they would remind me that they whip me because they Love me
But because I was young
I just thought they Loved me too much and too long...
Now I can see they loved me more than enough.

I'm just sitting, thinking, and thanking God for my parents...

And their sacrifice
I remember when my father took out the time
To teach me how to ride my first bike
And I remember the time he sacrificed his body
With a bad hip
Crammed with so much pain
He played me one-on-one in a basketball game
And for that
My gratitude is insane!
And my mother
is the main reason for my success
Because she sacrificed her rest
To make sure we had the best
Coming up we always stayed happy

And moms made sure my sister's hair never stayed Nappy
And the thing that really hits me is that

Even while my moms fought for her life
She continued to sacrifice her life
To make sure we lived a good and safe life.

I'm just Sitting, Thinking, and Thanking God for my parents...

And who they are to me
Gifts from God to me
Love wrapped in flesh
They are two individuals that taught us not to get trapped in mess
Always encouraging us to strive to give God our best
They are quick to live and slow to rest
Quick to Give and slow to receive
Slow to doubt and quick to believe
Yes!
My parents mean so much to me
My parents taught us less with their mouths
And more with their lifestyles
And now
That I am a Parent with my own family

I can now be the parent that my moms and father are to my sisters and
Me.

I'm just sitting, thinking, and thanking God for my parents...

Preacher's kid

In life we go through many different changes
So allow me to share with you a few of my life changes
And the effects of evil communication
In four phases...

"Choose Ye this Day!"
I heard it from a preacher as he began to say...
"Choose Ye this Day!"
I said I heard it from a preacher as he began to say...

Phase one
And as I began to sit back and wonder
What this man is talking about
And what is the meaning of the words proceeding
Out of his mouth
Because he's talking like he could see through me
And if he can he should see that I aint done no dirt
Because my father is a preacher man
And on top of that
I was raised in church
And I got enough knowledge
I just graduated from high school

And I'm on my way to college
And I'm staying on campus too…
Now wait
There's a slight hesitation
Because
If I've done the right calculations
College, campus, add the freedom
Equals an increase in temptation…

<u>Phase two</u>
It was the first day of school
And I witnessed students doing things
That I just don't do, can't do, and won't do
Far from being finished
I told myself that I was strong enough to be amongst it
I told myself that I was strong enough to be amongst it
Yes
I failed to realize that darkness and light could not reside
In the same place
But if you could look at my face
You would see that I know my thought process
Was out of place
At the time,
But I chose to follow

So just listen and pay close attention as I
continue to press rewind
While my story gets hollow and
Deep

<u>Phase three</u>

I fooled myself into thinking that the sin on
campus
Would not phase me
For I was not moved by the drugs
Or the pressure to drink
I even disliked the smoke aroma to soar pass
me
And I never embraced the thought of me having
a hangover
While hugging the toilet seat
You see
I was me
I was only excited about being home free
So I continued to be in the midst of it
I said I continued to be in the midst of it
As my understanding decreased
I neglected my soul while believing that
If I continue to 'Just Say NO'
My light would glow bright like the sun light
But instead I had no effect on the eyes of the
walking dead
Because my light was dim, and more like the
moon light
This leads me to...

Phase four

Hanging out with the in-crowd
While they were free and acting wild
And me 'Just Saying No'
Was becoming a bore
Ignorant to the reality of me
Choosing to be
In the midst of it
Made me no different from them...
We... Us...
You see I went to the clubs
Didn't drink
So I thought I was a righteous man
Because I danced with a bottle of H2o in my hand
(Even though I was doing the unrighteous dance)
Baggy pants, baggy shirts, I fitted right in
No one could perceive that I was raised in church
And as I compromised
I fed my eyes
With
Nice hips and thighs
And became hypnotized
By the tight pants and mini skirts
Inside of me
Lust began to arise
For I said "No" long enough to certain things
Like drugs, alcohol, and smoke

And began to say "Yes" to Sex
I chose to Follow
I sat in on vain conversations about sex and violence
I thought I was being strong by staying silent
And holding back all comments
Only giving laughs and sighs
While in the back of my mind
I would hurt
For I knew I had nothing in common
Because I was raised in church...
But I continued to be in the midst of it
But I continued to be in the midst of it
And eventually my church dedication faded away
And I then became overtaken by Fornication and Masturbation...
And I couldn't believe that sin crept in
(Even though I invited her in)
So rapidly through gained attention
And
I feel the need to mention
That all of this took place within the first week...
Now this story just became deep
It don't take long to get overtaken by wrong
Please Believe Me
Two years later from that first week
I Gave Christ all of Me
Thankful now because He Forgave Me
And

I'm writing you, to help you see
That you can't compromise with sin
And expect to make it in
For this life is short
And Death is near
So be who you are
Preacher's Kid
Choose Ye this Day
To be Bold enough to uphold the blood stained
Banner
And be not deceived because
Evil communication
Corrupts good manners

I Found Love

I found Love, I found Love, I found Love
Love has chosen me to be a habitation for it to dwell in
I have been endowed with love
This causes me to love those who don't even deserve to be loved
This love has shown me to love, love, and love
Until my heart becomes soar
And this love that dwells inside of me
Will cause me to live for eternity
This means I will never reach a point when I can't love anymore
Even if my heart does become soar
I am so Happy, my soul is finally satisfied
I found Love
So now I can see
I can now see
The tricks of the enemy
I can now see that there is nothing in between Love and Hate
This Love feels so good
I just want it to use me,
To draw you,
So that it can dwell in you
So that we all can relate
I Found Love, I found Love, I found Love
Love has been taking me by the hand

Love is my best friend
Love have been teaching me how to
Truly Love my natural friends
Love is teaching me how to Love my associates
I found Love
Love is Teaching me how to believe
I believe that even when my close Brother
Takes a dagger and stabs me in the back
I can still Love him back
And Provoke him to
Take the dagger out of my back
And Love me back
Love has made me to endure
All the tests and trials that come my way
Day by day
Fret I will not
Because Love has enlightened me
That I'm not here to stay
I Found Love, I found Love, I found Love
Love is everlasting
Love is not puffed up
But lifts up
Those who are messed up
From their head to their toes
Yes!
Those whom Love has chosen
I found Love

All in the right places
Love has no respect of faces
My gratitude keeps rising because love is not racist
Love has given me Patience
Even for those who are racist
Love has given me love for all races
Yes!
I found Love, I must confess!
I found Love, I'm Blessed Because
I found Love, I found Love, I found Love, I found...
God
And true this can only be
Because He- first –Loved-ME...
I found Love

WAR CRY

Introduction

This poem was birthed after the death of my cousin, Moonie. And may he Rest In Peace...

WAR CRY

The cycle is in **rotation**
The captain of the ship is **SATAN**
Im done Crying
Im **Hatin**
Not flesh and blood, not even the **situation**
Im hatin,
Satan

Revenge is mine says the **Lord**
So everybody who can hear my **voice**,
make the wisest **choice**
And stop trying to live Life by the **sword**
Because you will Die by the **sword.**
This Is **War**!
And I'm fighting back!
With Love...
So people **listen**
Please pay close **attention**
This is not a poem,
These are strictly words
That are God **given**
To **me**
As my Heart **bleeds**
My heart **pleads**, with those out there running
the death race on those vain and empty **streets**
My heart **pleads** with those
Church folks trying too hard to sit in the

Judgment **seat**
My heart bleeds as I sit and **think**
About how it so **seems**
As if the message of **prosperity** out- weighs
The gospel of Jesus **Christ**
Most church folks care more about your money than your **life**
Preachers are quick to tell the truth
After they get **caught** in a **Lie**
Living a Sinful **life**
We were **taught**, that either you come clean or stay away Dirty
This **thing** is Black or **white**, there is no in-**between**

And it's amazing to **me** how people try to **compromise** to save **lives**
They say, *"That If you keep young folks* ***Dancing***
And use Hip-Hop music and call it ***Gospel***
We have a better ***chance*** *to gain their attention"*
(pause)
I call that!
Another **Gospel**
Created by **Satan**

Truth **is**
We don't know where death **is**

I just lost my little cousin **again**
The same **way**
Satan used my **people**, to kill my **people**, with guns and **violence**
Let us continue to **pray**
Because this is **non-sense**
And **hear this**
We as a people make Satan's Job even simple
I say this
Fearless

When will this blood bath **End**?
I don't **know**!
But I chose to take this **road**
I stand **bold**!
Flat footed against all **violence**
I've made the choice to break all my **silence**
I'm -done -being -**Quiet**

This is a war **cry**!!!
No time to be asking the Lord **Why**
When we already know the **answer**
This hate **crime** starts at home
And it spreads out into the **streets** like **cancer**

Please don't judge me and think that I'm trying to preach
But instead
Close your **eyes** and **see** what I **see**
Because

You might **see** a foolish **Thug**
I see a Lost young man with no **guidance**
In dire need of his Fathers **Love**
His home is **divided**

You might see a hot headed, promiscuous
female that won't **listen**
I see a lost young lady searching for Her
Father's **attention**

You might see a church full of hypocrites and **all**
I see a building, filled with people
Lead by a pastor that has not truly been **called**

You see a city that is decreasing and destined to
fall
I **see** a **citywaiting** for us Men to stand **tall** and
take **heed**
Get back to bending **knees** and stop rejecting
the **Call**
To **lead**

So I say to **all** who are truly free from **sin**
Parents, aunties, uncles, churches, families, and
friends
Keep your head up and let's stay Focus to the
end
Because in the **End**,
We **win**
For we are more than just **human**

We are God's **Children**

For this a War Cry!
For us to do less **talkin** and more **walkin**
Let's match our **preaching** by increasing our **teaching**
Let's close our **mouths**, sit **down**
And start listening to this lost **generation**
So that we can kill the root to all this **hatred**
Let's start leading by example
Less with our **mouths**, and more with our **lifestyles**

This is a war cry!
To all the people of God to stop **trying** to be right
And start being who you say you **are Christ like**

This is a Love cry!
To all my young people hurting and filled with so much **Hate**
Jesus the **Christcried, died**, and rose **again** for **you**
And he can change your life **today** if you let Him In, **Truth**
Don't wait because tomorrow might be too **late**

This is a War cry!
To many

Churches here in **Flint**
If you want to save this city
Let the Holy Ghost lead **again**
But first,
REPENT!!

This is a Love Cry!
This is a war cry!
For everyone who can hear these **words**
Let's come **together** as a union and Arise Above
all this Mess **caused** by hatred
Like **birds** that fly and flock through the
toughest **weather**

This-Is-War!
I say it **againBoldly**
Standing free from **sin**
Grateful that God **chose me**
I stand against **Satan**,
The cycle
And it's **rotation**
I stand Against **Satan operating**
In any man, woman, boy or **girl too**
Because greater is **He** that is within **me** than **he**
that is in the **World**
And possibly
In You!...
Lord
Hear my Cry
Satan

Hear me Roar!
And mark my word
This Is WAR!
AND IM FIGHTING BACK!!!
WITH LOVE…

Uncle Robert

Psalms 37
Let us know that the decisions we make as God's people
Will be seen by many people
This is why I decided to inform with a poem
Many people about a Man

You see
This man
Is dear to my heart
'I hold near'
This man from the start
Has been there for me
Way back to when I was swinging my feet
While sitting in a car seat
This man has other children
And he continued to treat me as his own
His home
Was my home away from home
This has great meaning because this man is a great father
Stored inside of him is a father's love that goes down Ocean Deep
And I believe
His love travels deeper than a submarine
This man is a Warrior
Satan has tried to take this man's life

By piercing his heart
With countless fiery darts
Simple and plain
This man has gone through some tough thangs
That would cause another man to go insane
But this man is a Warrior
He keeps fighting, pushing, and living
The Love he has for his dear children
Is used as ammunition
He never runs out
No doubt
God has given this Man the strength to fight
To gain all the Glory out of his life
For his life can be used to draw others to Christ
This man's life and love for his children
Is a testimony necessary to be heard by millions
And I end this with a chant
While I stand to my feet...

For he overcame many adversities
All because of God's grace and mercy

For he overcame many adversities
All because of God's grace and mercy

For he overcame many adversities
All because of God's grace and mercy

DEACON

A Deacon is the name of a man
Chosen to carry out God's Plan
He is
Dedicated to do God's will no matter who comes
No matter who goes
Because he knows
He is a man whom God has chose
He is
Educatedin God's word
Assertive when he speaks
Eager to teach
Has no concern for souls being judged
But a great concern for souls being reached
He is
An Awesomeindividual
Since the God he serves is Awesome
Causing him to speak awesome words
Walk in awesome wisdom
And talk with awesome love
Always speaks what he practice
And if he is despitefully abused
He gives an awesome reaction
He is
Committed to serving his Lord and Master
He stays loyal and faithful to his leader or pastor

He positions his life
Under the authority of Jesus Christ
Committing to live the truth before those
Who may cross his path
Because he has no desire to experience God's wrath
He is
Outstanding
Because he continues to stand out of the crowd
That chooses to run loose and wild
As he stays mindful that he is more than just human
He knows he is God's child
He is
Nicebecause he has obtained respect for all
With spiritual meekness
He picks his brother up when he sees him fall
Since he understands that Jesus Christ
Has paid the price
For him to be spiritually nice
He is a
Dedicated, **E**ducated, **A**wesome, **C**ommitted, **O**utstanding, and **N**ice
Man whom the Holy God has chose
Which lets us know
That He is
Full of the Holy Ghost

A Holy Ghost filled man driven by the inward passion
Better explained with one phrase…
Less Talk and More Action

Fabulous at 50

Look in the sky
It's an angel that flies
And this angel is in disguise
Because she is dressed in Beautiful brown flesh
Look at her eyes shine with truth at her best
Blessed with a tongue that speaks words so powerful
That if you listen
You will live life long and not sorrowful
She will increase your hope and make you less doubtful
She is
My Momma
She lives
A life full of Joy and less drama
I'm excited while thinking about her
I'm even more elated while writing about her
She is
My Momma, my friend, my counselor, my hero...
Now let's go
For this is only my intro

To express myself and bless you
With my point of view
Of the woman of this day
My Momma
First name Donna, Last name Washington,

Middle name Faye
Eager to celebrate the dedication she has shown
and given
To her family and friends throughout the years
Blood sweat and Tears
Is the manifestation of the hard work she has
Put in

Beautiful
But she knows how to wear a frown
Only when confusion and sin comes around
Then and now
Wow
Is the word that proceeds out of my mouth
As I continue to watch her Kingdom lifestyle
How
She enjoys dressing to impress
Herself
Because she aint worried about everyone else
And that's real talk
Which is something that she likes to do
Everyday she tries to meet somebody new
And she's good at it too
Remember
The day when she met you
It was not a coincidence
For that day was meant

To be
For us
To celebrate God's present
With Love
And because of her we can lift
Him up
A little bit higher
Don't worry
She won't get jealous because
Lifting up Christ is her number one desire
She live to give God the glory
Yes
She is a woman of faith
Through faith she stood her ground
Cried out loud
And made death a bow face and turn away
She overcame
Now allow me to explain with a quick and
powerful phrase…

"The doctors gave her three days,
But she continued to praise His Name
And overcame"…

Ending
My momma is my example in being
Real and steady
At all times
She is my wife's example in treating me right
At all times

(Just ask my deddy)
She is always giving, which is why she always uplifts me
Growing up she was the only one who understood me
She loves her children so much that it fills me
With Glee
Her love and compassion heals me
The bigger picture she pushes me to see
And I hope you all can now see
Through this heartfelt poetry
The reason why my mom is
And
Always will be
FABULOUS-AT-FIFTY

<u>Unity</u>

Genesis 1:26
God Said!!!
Let **Us make** man in **our** image...
Us----Our-----Power= Unity

Without Unity
You and me
Would not even be here at this hour
So let's take the time to acknowledge and praise
Our savior for being united with our creator
Who keeps us uplifted by his Spirit
He keeps me gifted to speak and say
The word for this day
That will stay and stick with you for longer than one day...
Unity
U-N-I-T-Y

Confession
We were made under the influence of unity
This is why we have two legs that can only take us into one
Direction
And two eyes that can only focus on one object
Life is already hectic

So without unity
There is no need for you and me
Please see that the necessity of unity should not be neglected
Success is a guarantee
And to be blessed
We must all together get back to bending knees
And believe
God to increase peace and wisdom so that we can be
More effective in winning souls that comes in
Straight from the violent streets
And we must know that nothing can stand between
Us and our savior
So let's continue to fight together to obtain and maintain
The right behavior
Mannerism, conversation, hospitality
Let us all not connect negativity with reality
Because spirituality is reality
So let's get real
Let's put an end to neglecting the presence of
Our Brothers and Sisters
Let's all come together
Think together, cry together, and live life
Together

What's yours is mine, and what's mine is
yours... Spiritually
If you got peace, I got peace
If you got blessed, I got blessed
If you got love, I got love
And we all can use our hands and our life to lift
up Christ without
Hesitation
To share the good news of our
Salvation
Not only with our mouths but also with our
Lifestyles
Unity is the word for this day
Unity is the word for this day
So let's walk and talk in harmony
Join this union
And let's participate in sweet communion
Us as a unit makes us more than just human
We are God's children
And this union consists of more than us eating
Together
Let's all pray together more
Fast together more
Witness together more
And study together more
So that we can all over come all forms of
Weather
Through the Power of...
Genesis 1:26
God Said!!

Let **Us Make** man in **Our** image
Us-Our-Power...
UNITY

Walls

Behind these walls
There's a war going on
We are stuck in-between
Behind the scene
And we are all alone
Fighting and waiting
For that special someone to come and make us free
So that we can be
Not me, but you
And
Not you, but me
Ready to let the whole world see
The real me
The real you
And let them know that there is nobody like you
Not even a few
For you are
One of a kind
No one can come in
To expose your own mind
Pleas listen
No one can read
What you have not yet written
No one can finish
Your own sentence
Please listen because…

It's time to Break these walls down!!

Now
Let's go deeper
Let me be the first to let you know
That these walls are see-through
You can only hide from people
We are losing our places
Other roles have been taken
Because of the fears of being forsaken
By our peers
Tired of others hating
Tired of trying to relate and
Finding our selves trying to please fake friends
When will this end?
When will we finally dig deep
And leave the shallow end?
Let's take a bold step in being our selves
And stretch out and reach for the top shelves
And unleash
The power that's behind being unique
That also abides in you and me
So that we can stand strong
Instead of standing alone
In the power of Unity

<u>I'm about to Break these walls down!</u>

Now
I believe these walls will be broken
The joker will stop jokin
And the harlot will become free
From selling her body for a vain fee
And you may call me insane
But I really mean this
That
The pimp will take his cane
And give it to someone who really needs it
And take his hands that he has used to abuse
And raise them high into the sky
And surrender unto the Lord Jesus Christ
With a heart full of so much gratitude
After he understands
That he himself has been given a second chance

<u>I believe that these walls will be broken</u>

And the abusive husband will stop choking
And start loving his wife
And the wife will stop bickering and nagging
And start being sweet and nice
And the back stabber
Will take his invisible knife
And use it to help break these walls down

And start using his hands and living his life
To push others to their highest potential

<u>I believe these walls will be broken</u>

The hopeless will start hoping
And the helpless will start helping
Even
The dope Fein to stop doping

<u>I believe these walls will be broken</u>

The right decisions will be chosen
The poser will stop posing
The deceiver will stop deceiving
The liar will stop lying
And the cheater will stop cheating

<u>I believe these walls will be broken</u>

Men will be men
And women will be women
Young men will be young men
And young ladies will be young ladies
Boys will be boys
And girls will be girls
Fathers will be fathers

And Mothers will be mothers
Friends will be friends
Teachers will be teachers
And
Leaders will be leaders
You will be you
I will be me
And
We all will stand strong
Instead of standing alone
And grow as a people
In the power of unity
But first...
With the Love of Jesus Christ
We-Got-To-Break-These-Walls-Down...

Blind

Young people need to realize how powerful You
are
And how
Great it is to be covered by Your blood
They need to be aware of
The blessings that You pour down from heaven
above
They need to see
That You are full of everlasting Love
And
How You can allow them to live
Life abundantly
Like a high flying dove
But
They are blinded by Satan's tricks
In which he has created to take away
Their focus from
All the truth being taught today
The fear is not there and they can't see
The reality of burning in hell for eternity
Distraction is everywhere through things
Like Hip-hop and R&B
Which was created not to Glorify thee
But they can't see...

Thank God for the Way I was Brought Up

Away with the baby steps
It's time to make a big step
Taking the responsibility of surviving on my own
Without my parents there to watch me
Because
Pretty soon I will be free
Free to do whatever I please
Party all night, watch TV
I don't have to worry about no curfew
Cleaning up after myself everyday
Parenting discipline does not exist
Only choices, success, and failure
But
Thank God for the way I was brought up…

Someone

It's nice to find someone who only knows how to be genuine
Someone who I can relate to
Someone who like sports like I do
And can remain feminine
Someone who is not like most women
It's nice to talk to someone on the phone for hours
When it feels less than an hour
Talking about everything from natural to spiritual power
Someone who I can actually see myself with in the near future
Someone who can teach me a lot about anything
And she's not even my school teacher
It's nice to find
Someone who I can easily express myself around no matter what
Someone I can call my baby and tell her that it is her who I am crazy for
Someone who can tell me the truth even when it hurts
And whose patience is not shorter than a mini skirt
Someone who knows how to appreciate a good guy
Someone who does not practice telling lies

I always thought it would take a long time
To find someone like this
But I guess I am wrong
This is the one time when I am wrong
(And it feels so good)
I can write a long happy song
Plain and simple
Simple and plain
This someone gives me feelings that I just can't explain
Maybe I will one day
But for now
This poem is good enough
So I hope you like it because that someone is...
You

Contact Page

The author is available for speaking engagements, book signings, personal appearances, seminars, special events and media interviews. He can be reached by using the contact information below.

Ministry on Paper (M.O.P)

Lawrence Washington Jr.

The Poet Minister

The Church of God

1513 Kent St.

Flint, MI

lawrencewashington21@yahoo.com

CPSIA information can be obtained at www.ICGtesting.com
Printed in the USA
BVOW072348250112

281398BV00001B/2/P

9 780984 936014